James Otiss Speech On The Writs Of Assistance, 1906

James Otiss

In the interest of creating a more extensive selection of rare historical book reprints, we have chosen to reproduce this title even though it may possibly have occasional imperfections such as missing and blurred pages, missing text, poor pictures, markings, dark backgrounds and other reproduction issues beyond our control. Because this work is culturally important, we have made it available as a part of our commitment to protecting, preserving and promoting the world's literature. Thank you for your understanding.

PRICE, 10 CENTS.

American History Leaflets

COLONIAL AND CONSTITUTIONAL.

EDITED BY

ALBERT BUSHNELL HART AND EDWARD CHANNING,

OF HARVARD UNIVERSITY.

NO. 33.

JAMES OTIS'S SPEECH ON THE
WRITS OF ASSISTANCE.
1761.

PARKER P. SIMMONS

1906

Entered at the New York Post Office as second class matter.
COPYRIGHT, 1902, BY A. LOVELL & COMPANY.

American History Leaflets.

COLONIAL AND CONSTITUTIONAL.

No. 33.

JAMES OTIS'S SPEECH ON WRITS OF ASSISTANCE.

1761.

CONTENTS OF THIS NUMBER.

1. *Extract from Gray's Article in Quincy's Reports.*
2. *John Adams's Notes of Otis's Speech.*
3. *Gridley's Argument for the Writs from Keith's Note-Book.*
4. *Extract from Tudor's Otis describing the Occasion.*
5. *The Speech as printed in Tudor's Otis.*
6. *Tudor's concluding Remarks.*

James Otis's speech on the Writs of Assistance is conveniently regarded as the first in the chain of events which led directly and irresistibly to revolution and independence. It marks the tone of public opinion in Massachusetts in 1761, as Patrick Henry's Speech in the Parson's Cause two years later gives evidence of the condition of public opinion in Virginia in 1763.

Present knowledge of Otis's great speech is derived entirely from minutes of the evidence taken by John Adams — not yet admitted to the bar. The manuscript of these or a copy of it was stolen from Adams's desk and printed in the *Worcester Spy* for April 29, 1773. Minot printed the *Spy* version in his *Massachusetts* (II. 89-99). The account in Tudor's *Life of Otis*, which is here reprinted, is practically the work of Adams — when an old man. Tudor's book was published in 1823; Adams and Tudor were in correspondence on this subject in 1818. This account probably was written between 1818 and 1823. Among the Adams papers are some notes of Otis's Argument. These are printed in Adams's Works (II. 125), in Quincy's *Reports* (pp. 469-476), and again here. A "Note-book" made by Israel Keith contains a longer version of Gridley's Argument than "Adams's Notes," or the "*Spy* Article." It is here reprinted from Quincy's

Copyright, 1902, by A. LOVELL & COMPANY.

Reports. As Keith was nine years old in 1761 the minutes could not have been made by him. Possibly they represent an early copy of Adams's original minutes. The portion containing Gridley's Speech is here reprinted from Quincy's *Reports.* The whole subject of Writs of Assistance is there most admirably studied by Horace Gray, Jr., Esq., later Chief Justice of Massachusetts and now Associate Justice of the Supreme Court of the United States. His concluding paragraph is here reproduced.

No apology is needed for reprinting the long extracts from Tudor's *Otis.* The book is a classic in Revolutionary biography. Many of the opinions and assertions made in it have not borne the brunt of modern research. But all in all it is a masterly work. The comparison of Adams's minutes taken at the time and his account of the matter a half a century later gives one an admiration for the tenacity of the venerable statesman's memory, and also an added distrust of "old men's recollections as a source of history."

The best brief account of the various forms of Otis's Speech is that by Dr. S. A. Green in the Massachusetts Historical Society's *Proceedings,* 2d Series, VI. 190. The full titles of Quincy's and Tudor's works are as follows: Josiah Quincy, Jr., *Reports of Cases argued and adjudged in the Superior Court of Judicature of the Province of Massachusetts Bay between 1761 and 1772,* Boston, 1865 — the general editorial work was done by Samuel M. Quincy; William Tudor, *The Life of James Otis of Massachusetts,* Boston, 1823. For other references see Channing and Hart, *Guide to the Study of American History,* § 134.

1. Extract from Gray's Article in Quincy's Reports.

A careful examination of the subject compels the conclusion that the decision of *Hutchinson* and his associates has been too strongly condemned as illegal: and that there was at least reasonable ground for holding, as matter of mere law, that the British Parliament had power to bind the Colonies; that even a statute contrary to the Constitution could not be declared void by the judicial Courts; that by the English statutes, as practically construed by the Courts in England, Writs of Assistance might be general in form; that the Superior Court of Judicature of the Province had the power of the English Court of Exchequer; and that the Writs of Assistance prayed for, though contrary to the spirit of the English Constitution, could hardly be refused by a Provincial Court, before general warrants had been condemned in England, and before the Revolution had actually begun in America. The remedy adopted by the Colonies was to throw off the yoke of Parliament; to confer on the judiciary the power to declare unconstitutional statutes void; to declare general warrants unconstitutional in express terms; and thus to put an end here to general Writs of Assistance. — Quincy's *Reports*, 540.

Reprinted by permission of Messrs. Little, Brown & Co.

2. John Adams's Report of Otis's Speech.*

GRIDLEY. — The Constables distraining for Rates. more inconsistent with Eng. Rts. & liberties than Writts of assistance. And Necessity, authorizes both.

Thatcher. I have searched, in all the ancient Repertories, of Precedents, in Fitzherberts Natura Brevium, and in the Register (Q. w^t ye Reg. is) and have found no such Writt of assistance as this Petition prays. — I have found two Writts of ass. in the Reg. but they are very difft, from ye Writt prayd for. —

In a Book, intituled the Modern Practice of the Court of Exchequer there is indeed one such Writt, and but one.

By ye Act of Pal^t. any other private Person, may as well as a Custom House Officer, take an officer, a Sheriff, or Constable, &c and go into any Shop, Store &c & seize: any Person authorized by such a Writt, under the Seal of the Court of Exchequer, may, not Custom House Officers only. — Strange. — Only a temporary thing.

The most material Question is, whether the Practice of the Exchequer, will warrant this Court in granting the same.

The Act impowers all the officers of ye Revenue to enter and

---

* This report, which has been once published in 2 John Adams's Works, 521-523, is by the courteous permission of *Mr. Charles Francis Adams* here reprinted as exactly as possible, with the original paragraphs, spelling, and punctuation, from the MS. notes of *John Adams*, who was present at the argument, though he was not admitted as a barrister until the 14th of November following. 2 John Adams's Works, 124 and note, 133. 10 *Ib.* 245. Rec. 1761, fol. 239. The only other contemporaneous report is an enlargement of this. *Vide infra*, 477, note 39.

The elaborate narrative given more than half a century afterwards by *Adams* to *Tudor*, who printed an abstract of it as the argument of *Otis* in this case, is rather a recollection of the sentiments of the colonists between 1761 and 1766. 10 John Adams's Works, 232-362 and note. Tudor's *Life of Otis*, 68-86. 4 Bancroft's *Hist. U. S.* 417, note. *Ante*, 409, 417. It would seem to have been written by *Adams* without even referring to his own notes; for it substitutes Rastall's Entries for Registrum Brevium; and asserts that no precedent could be found of a writ of assistance to a custom house officer — in direct opposition to all the counsel in the case, as reported by himself in the text. 10 John Adams's Works, 322, 342. He seems also to attribute to *Otis* his own argument, seven years later, in the case of *The Liberty*, *ante*, 460, 461. 10 John Adams's Works, 348, 349.

seise in the Plantations, as well as in England. 7. & 8 W^m. 3, C. 22, § 6, gives the same as 13. & 14. of C. gives in England. The Ground of Mr Gridleys ag^t. is this, that his Court has the Power of the Court of Exchequer. — But This Court has renounced the Chancery Jurisdiction, w^h the Exchequer has in Cases where either Party, is ye Kings Debtor. — Q. into y^t Case.

In Eng. all Informations of uncusted or prohibited Importations, are in ye Exchequer. — So y^t ye Custom House officers are the officers of y^t Court. — under the Eye, and Direction of the Barons

The Writ of Assistance is not returnable. — If such seisure were brot before your Honours, youd often find a wanton Exercise of their Power.

At home, ye officers, seise at their Peril, even with Probable Cause. —

Otis. This Writ is against the fundamental Principles of Law. — The Priviledge of House. A Man, who is quiet, is as secure in his House, as a Prince in his Castle — notwithstanding all his Debts, & civil processes of any Kind. — But

For flagrant Crimes, and in Cases of great public Necessity, the Priviledge may be incrohd [incroached?] on. — For Felonies an officer may break, upon Proscess, and oath. — i.e. by a Special Warrant to search such an House, sworn to be suspected, and good Grounds of suspicion appearing.

Make oath cor^m Ld. Trea^{er}, or Exchequer, in Eng^d or a Magistrate here, and get a Special Warrant, for ye public good, to infringe the Priviledge of House.

Genl. Warrant to search for Felonies. Hawk. Pleas Crown. — every petty officer from the highest to ye lowest, and if some of 'em are uncom̃ others are uncomm̃. Gouv^t Justices used to issue such perpetual Edicts. (Q. with w^t particular Reference?)

But one Precedent, and y^t in ye Reign of C. 2 when Star Chamber Powers, and all Powers but lawful & useful Powers were pushed to Extremity. —

The authority of this Modern Practice of the Court of Exchequer. — it has an Imprimatur. — But w^t may not have? — It may be owing to some ignorant Clerke of ye Exchequer.
MARCH FIFTEENTH 18.

But all Precedents and this am'g ye Rest are under ye Control of yᵉ Principles of Law. Ld. Talbot. better to observe the known Principles of Law yⁿ any one Precedent, tho in the House of Lords. —

As to Acts of Parliament. an Act against the Constitution is void: an Act against natural Equity is void: and if an Act of Parliament should be made, in the very Words of this Petition, it would be void. The Executive Courts must pass such Acts into disuse — 8. Rep. 118. from Viner. — Reason of yᵉ Com͞ Law to control an Act of Parliament. — Iron Manufacture. noble Lord's Proposal, yᵗ we should send our Horses to Eng. to be shod. —

If an officer will justify under a Writ he must return it. 12ᵗʰ. Mod. 396. — perpetual Writ.

Stat. C. 2. We have all as good Rt to inform as Custom House officers — & every Man may have a general, irreturnable Commission to break Houses. —

By 12. of C. on oath before Lᵈ Treasurer, Barons of Exchequer, or Chief Magistrate to break with an officer. — 14ᵗʰ C. to issue a Warrant requiring sheriffs &c to assist the officers to search for Goods not entrd, or prohibtd; 7 & 8ᵗʰ W. & M. gives Officers in Plantations same Powers with officers in England. —

Continuance of Writts and Proscesses, proves no more nor so much as I grant a special Writ of ass. on special oath, for specl Purpose. —

Pew indorsd Warrant to Ware. — Justice Walley searc'd House. Law Prov. Bill in Chancery. —this Court confined their Chancery Power to Revenue &c. — Quincy's *Reports*, 469–476.

Reprinted by permission of Messrs. Little, Brown & Co.

3. Gridley's Argument for the Writs from Keith's Note-book.

"Mʳ. *Gridley*. I appear on the behalf of Mʳ. Cockle and others, who pray 'that as they cannot fully exercise their Offices in such a manner as his Majesty's Service and their Laws in such cases require, unless your Honors who are vested with the power of a Court of Exchequer for this Province will please to grant them Writs of Assistance. They therefore pray that they & their Deputies may be aided in the Execution of their

Offices by Writs of Assistance under the Seal of this Court and in legal form, & according to the Usage of his Majesty's Court of Exchequer in Great Britain.'

"May it please your Honors, it is certain it has been the practice of the Court of Exchequer in England, and of this Court in this Province, to grant Writs of Assistance to Custom House Officers. Such Writs are mentioned in several Acts of Parliament, in several Books of Reports; & in a Book called the Modern Practice of the Court of Exchequer, We have a Precedent, a form of a Writ, called a Writ of Assistance for Custom house Officers, of which the following a few years past to Mr Paxton under the Seal of this Court, & tested by the late Chief Justice Sewall is a literal Translation." [Here follows the writ printed *ante*, 404.]

"The first Question therefore for your Honors to determine is, whether this practice of the Court of Exchequer in England (which it is certain, has taken place heretofore, how long or short a time soever it continued) is legal or illegal. And the second is, whether the practice of the Exchequer (admitting it to be legal) can warrant this Court in the same practice.

"In answer to the first, I cannot indeed find the Original of this Writ of Assistance. It may be of very antient, to which I am inclined, or it may be of modern date. This however is certain, that the Stat. of the 14th Char. 2nd has established this Writ almost in the words of the Writ itself. 'And it shall be lawful to & for any person or persons *authorised by Writ of Assistance under the seal of his Majesty's Court of Exchequer* to take a Constable, Headborough, or other public Officer, inhabiting near unto the place, & in the day time to enter & go into any house, Shop, Cellar, Warehouse, room, or any other place, and in case of Resistance, to break open doors, Chests, Trunks & other Package, & there to seize any kind of Goods or Merchandize whatever prohibited, and to put the same into his Majesty's Warehouse in the Port where Seizure is made.'

"By this act & that of 12 Char. 2nd all the powers in the Writ of Assistance mentioned are given, & it is expressly said, the persons shall be authorised by Writs of Assistance under the seal of the Exchequer. Now the Books in which we should expect to find these Writs, & all that relates to them are Books of Precedents, & Reports in the Exchequer, which are extremely scarce in this Country; we have one, & but one that treats of Exchequer matters, and that is called the 'Modern practice of the Court of Exchequer,' & in this Book we find one Writ of Assistance, translated above. Books of Reports have commonly the Sanction of all the Judges, but books of Precedents never have more than that of the Chief Justice. Now this Book has the Imprimatur of Wright, who was Chief Justice of the King's Bench, and it was wrote by Brown, whom I esteem the best Collector of Precedents; I have Two Volumes of them by him, which I esteem the best except Rastall & Coke. But we have a further proof of the legality of these Writs, & of the settled practice at home of allowing them; because by the Stat. 6th Anne which continues all Processes & Writs after the Demise of the Crown, *Writs of Assistance are continued among the Rest.*

"It being clear therefore that the Court of Exchequer at home has a power by Law of granting these Writs, I think there can be but little doubt, whether this Court as a Court of Exchequer for this Province has this power. By the Statute of the 7th & 8th W. 3d, it is enacted 'that all the Officers for collecting and managing his Majesty's Revenue, and inspecting the Plantation Trade in any of the said Plantations, shall have the same powers &c. as are provided for the Officers of the Revenue in England; also to enter Houses, or Warehouses, to search for and seize any such Goods, & that the *like Assistance* shall be given to the said Officers as is the Custom in England."

"Now what is the Assistance which the Officers of the Revenue are to have here, which is like that they have in England? Writs of Assistance under the Seal of his Majesty's Court of Exchequer at home will not run here. They must therefore be under the Seal of this Court. For by the law of this Province 2 W. 3d Ch. 3 'there shall be a Superior Court '&c. over the whole Province &c. who shall have cognizance of 'all pleas &c. & generally of all other matters, as fully & '[amply] to all intents & purposes as the Courts of King's 'Bench, Common Pleas & *Exchequer* within his Majesty's 'Kingdom of England have or ought to have.'

"It is true the common privileges of Englishmen are taken away in this Case, but even their privileges are not so in cases of Crime and fine. 'Tis the necessity of the Case and the benefit of the Revenue that justifies this Writ. Is not the

Revenue the sole support of Fleets & Armies abroad, & Ministers at home? without which the Nation could neither be preserved from the Invasions of her foes, nor the Tumults of her own Subjects. Is not this I say infinitely more important, than the imprisonment of Thieves, or even Murderers? yet in these Cases 'tis agreed Houses may be broken open.

"In fine the power now under consideration is the same with that given by the Law of this Province to Treasurers towards Collectors & to them towards the subject. A Collector may when he pleases distrain my goods and Chattels, and in want of them arrest my person, and throw me instantly into Gaol. What! shall my property be wrested from me! — shall my Liberty be destroyed by a Collector, for a debt, unadjudged, without the common Indulgence and Lenity of the Law? So it is established, and the necessity of having public taxes effectually and speedily collected is of infinitely greater moment to the whole, than the Liberty of any Individual." — Quincy's *Reports*, 479–481.

Reprinted by permission of Messrs. Little, Brown & Co.

4. Tudor's Description of the Occasion — Chapter V.

Immediately after the conquest of Canada was completed, rumors were widely circulated, that a different system would be pursued, that the charters would be taken away, and the colonies reduced to royal governments. The offices [officers] of the customs began at once to enforce with strictness, all the acts of parliament regulating the trade of the colonies, several of which had been suspended, or become obsolete, and thus had never been executed at all. The good will of the colonists or their legislatures, was no longer wanted in the prosecution of the war; and the commissioners of the customs were permitted and directed to enforce the obnoxious acts. Governor Bernard, who was always a supporter of the royal prerogative, entered fully into these views, and shewed by his opinion, his appointments and his confidential advisers, that his object would be, to extend the power of the government to any limits, which the ministry might authorize.

The first demonstration of the new course intended to be pursued, was the arrival of an order in Council to carry into effect the Acts of trade, and to apply to the supreme judicature of the Province, for *Writs of Assistance*, to be granted to the officers of the customs. In a case of this importance there can be no doubt, that Mr. Paxton, who was at the head of the customs in Boston, consulted with the Government and all the crown officers, as to the best course to be taken. The result was, that he directed his deputy at Salem, Mr. Cockle, in November 1760, to petition the Superior Court, then sitting in that town, for "writs of assistance." Stephen Sewall who was the Chief Justice, expressed great doubt of the legality of such a writ, and of the authority of the Court to grant it. None of the other judges said a word in favour of it; but as the application was on the part of the Crown, it could not be dismissed without a hearing, which after consultation was fixed for the next term of the Court, to be held in February, 1761, at Boston, when the question was ordered to be argued. In the interval, Chief Justice Sewall died, and Lieutenant Governor Hutchinson was made his successor, thereby uniting in his person, the office of Lieutenant Governor with the emoluments of the commander of the castle, a member of the Council, Judge of Probate and Chief Justice of the Supreme Court! This appointment was unexpected and alarming to all reflecting minds, because it was evident that this important place could not have been given to a man who already held so many offices, some of which were quite incompatible with the place of Chief Justice, unless seconding the designs of government in all cases, was to be the excuse and the return for such extraordinary favours.

There were some circumstances of a personal kind connected with this appointment, that formed the ground work for very malicious and absurd misrepresentation. It was generally believed, that the place of Chief Justice, whenever it should become vacant, had been promised by Governor Shirley to James Otis's father, and that revenge for the disappointment was the cause of all his subsequent opposition. The language that was imputed to him by common report on this occasion, and which has been transmitted down, was according to one version, "that he would set the province in flames, though he perished in the fire" or according to another, in part of a well known line, *Acheronta movebo:* though neither of these speeches was ever authenticated. That Otis should have perceived, as clearly as any man, the impropriety and the danger of giving so many incongruous offices to one individual; that he would readily infer that the nomination could not have been made except from sinister views; that he should have felt disgust and indignation at the rapacity which could seek for such a monopoly of offices; that his quick and generous feelings should be roused at what he might consider an injury to a parent, is natural; but that his public career should have been forever guided by this transient emotion, is preposterous and impossible. It supposes a degree of dishonesty inconsistent with the powerful talents, which even his bitterest enemies acknowledged. If he had not been governed by principle, and taken the side which duty dictated, he was acting a part in sheer folly; for his talents, which led all the measures of opposition for a series of years, would have been retained on the opposite side at any price, and if his purpose had been only to revenge his father's cause, the certain mode of doing so, would have been to take part with the government. The motives of human conduct are seldom unmixed, and even the best men may, through the infirmities of nature, have some alloy with their noblest intentions. But there is no surer mark of a base and envious mind, than the belief, that narrow, sordid views, can be the exclusive means of giving to eminent men a lasting impulse in the career of public life.*

The mercantile part of the community was in a state of great anxiety, as to the result of this question. The officers of the Customs called upon Otis for his official assistance, as Advocate General, to argue their cause. But, as he believed these writs to be illegal and tyrannical, he refused. He would not prostitute his office to the support of an oppressive act; and with true delicacy and dignity, being unwilling to retain a station, in which he might be expected or called upon to argue in support of such odious measures, he resigned it, though the

---

* In writing upon this topic, Mr. Adams remarks: "It is provoking, and it is astonishing, and it is humiliating, to see how calumny sticks and is transmitted from age to age. Mr. —— is one of the last men that I should have expected to have swallowed that execrable lie, that Otis had no patriotism. The father was refused an office worth 1200 *l.* old tenor, or about 120 *l.* Sterling, and the refusal was no loss, for his practice at the bar was worth much more; for Colonel Otis was a lawyer in profitable practice, and his seat in the legislature gave him more power and more honour; for this refusal, the son resigned an office which he held from the Crown, worth twice that sum. The son must have been a most dutiful and affectionate child to the father; or rather most enthusiastically and frenzically affectionate."

situation was very lucrative, and if filled by an incumbent with a compliant spirit, led to the highest favours of government.

The merchants of Salem and Boston, applied to Mr. Pratt to undertake their cause, who was also solicited to engage on the other side; but he declined taking any part, being about to leave Boston for New York, of which province he had been appointed Chief Justice. They also applied to Otis and Thacher, who engaged to make their defence, and probably both of them without fees, though very great ones were offered. The language of Otis was, "in such a cause, I despise all fees."

Mr. Thacher, the colleague of Mr. Otis in this great cause, was at that time one of the heads of the bar in Boston, was a fine scholar, and possessed of much general learning. He received his degree at Cambridge in 1738; he first studied divinity, and began to follow a profession which had been that of his ancestors for several generations, but his voice being too weak for the pulpit, he gave it up to study law. His family was one of the most respectable in the Province, and his own character and manners were such, as to secure affection and esteem. Unassuming and affable in his deportment, of strict morality, punctual in his religious duties, and with sectarian attachments that made him, like a large majority of the people, look with jealousy and enmity on the meditated encroachments of the English hierarchy, he was in all these respects fitted to be popular. To these qualities he joined the most pure and ardent patriotism, and a quick preception [perception] of the views of those in power. He had been for a long time watchful of Hutchinson's ambition, but when he heard of his taking the place of Chief Justice, he no longer restrained his feelings, but on all occasions spoke of him with the contempt and indignation, that his selfishness and sinister conduct deserved. The opposition of Thacher gave the government great uneasiness: his disposition and habits secured public confidence, and while his moderation preserved him from the imputation of ambition, his learning and ability gave weight to his opinions, and prevented him from being considered as under the influence of others. Such a man might be esteemed an impartial umpire between the government and the people, and his example had naturally great weight with them. There was no pretext for assigning any unworthy motive for the part he took; and he was therefore the more to be dreaded. Mr.

Adams says, "they hated him worse than they did James Otis or Samuel Adams, and they feared him more, because they had no revenge for a father's disappointment of a seat on the Superior bench to impute to him, as they did to Otis."

He published some essays on the subject of an alteration proposed by Hutchinson relative to the value of gold and silver; in which controversy, as will be noticed hereafter, Otis took part on the same side. Thacher also wrote a pamphlet against the policy of the Navigation Act, and the Acts of Trade. This pamphlet is entitled "The Sentiments of a British American" printed in 1764. It is temperate, though earnest, and well written, the hardship and impolicy of these measures is very ably illustrated — His motto is a fable of Phœdrus, of which the close is a key to his sentiments —

> Ergo quid refert mea
> Cui serviam? clitellas dum portem meas.

He died of a pulmonary complaint, aggravated by his excessive anxiety respecting public affairs in 1765, after having been two years in the legislature from the town of Boston.*

The trial took place in the Council Chamber of the Old Town House, in Boston. This room was situated at the east end of that building, and like all the interior parts, has since undergone various alterations. At that time it was an imposing and elegant apartment, ornamented with two splendid full length portraits of Charles II. and James II. The Judges, in those days, in conformity to European practice, attached a part of their official dignity to a peculiar costume, which in later times they have here discarded. Their dress was composed of voluminous wigs, broad bands, and robes of scarlet

---

* "Not long before his death," says President Adams, "he sent for me, to commit to my care some of his business at the bar. I asked him whether he had seen the Virginia resolves: "Oh yes — they are men! they are noble spirits! It kills me, to think of the lethargy and stupidity that prevails here, I long to be out. I will go out — I will go out — I will go into Court and make a speech, which shall be read after my death, as my dying testimony against this infernal tyranny, which they are bringing upon us." Seeing the violent agitation into which it threw him, I changed the subject as soon as possible, and retired. He had been confined for some time. Had he been abroad among the people, he could not have complained so pathetically of the "lethargy and stupidity," for town and country were all alive; and in August, became active enough, and some of the people proceeded to unwarrantable excesses, which were more lamented by the patriots, than by their enemies. Mr. Thacher soon died, deeply lamented by all the friends of their country."

cloth. The judges were five in number, including Lieutenant Governor Hutchinson, who presided as Chief Justice. The room was filled with all the officers of government, and the principal citizens, to hear the arguments in a cause, that inspired the deepest solicitude.

The case was opened by Mr. Gridley, who argued it with much learning, ingenuity and dignity, urging every point and authority, that could be found after the most diligent search, in favour of the Custom house petition; making all his reasoning depend on this consideration — "if the parliament of Great Britain is the sovereign legislator of the British Empire."* He was followed by Mr. Thacher on the opposite side, whose reasoning was ingenious and able, delivered in a tone of great mildness and moderation. "But," in the language of President Adams, "Otis was a flame of fire; with a promptitude of classical allusions, a depth of research, a rapid summary of historical events and dates, a profusion of legal authorities, a prophetic glance of his eyes into futurity, and a rapid torrent of impetuous eloquence, he hurried away all before him. American Independence was then and there born. The seeds of patriots and heroes, to defend the *Non sine Diis animosus infans;* to defend the vigorous youth, were then and there sown. Every man of an immense crowded audience appeared to me to go away as I did, ready to take arms against Writs of Assistance. Then and there, was the first scene of the first act of opposition, to the arbitrary claims of Great Britain. Then and there, the child Independence was born. In fifteen years, i.e. in 1776, he grew up to manhood and declared himself free."

"There were no stenographers in those days," to give a complete report of this momentous harangue. How gladly

* This summary account of Mr. Gridley's argument is from President Adams's letters. In Minot's *History*, Vol. 2, p. 87. A short statement of his argument is given, which tends to shew that this writ was founded on statutes of the 12th and 14th of Charles II.; and the authority of the Supreme Court in this Province to grant it, was to be derived from the statute of the 7th and 8th of William III., which gave officers of the revenue in this country the same powers as officers in England — And that in the execution of their duty they should receive the *like assistance*. The obvious meaning of this seems to be, that an officer in case of necessity should have a right to call for the same support from those about him in pursuance of his duty. It seems a most st[r]ained and preposterous inference, to make the general term, *like assistance*, mean a special and odious process called a *writ of assistance*, invented in the worst times of the Stuart tyranny.

would be exchanged for it, a few hundred verbose speeches on some of the miserable, transient topics of the day, that are circulated in worthless profusion. Yet on this occasion, "the seeds were sown," and though some of them doubtless fell by the wayside or on stony places, others fell on good ground, and sprang up and increased and brought forth in due season, thirty, sixty and an hundred fold. Of the vigour of some of the soil that received this seed, the preceding quotation is a living and most eloquent proof. It indeed affords some compensation for the absence of contemporary records, and the subsequent neglect of this great leading transaction, that one of the hearers, after the lapse of sixty years, with all the authority which venerable age and illustrious services can confer, should have called the attention of his countrymen to the subject; and by a rare and felicitous force of memory, carrying back their regards over the course of two generations, have exhibited with a magical effect through the obscurity of time, an impressive and brilliant sketch, of one of the first struggles that led to their national existence.

5. Otis's Speech as printed in Tudor's "Otis" — Chapter VI.

Anxiety and expectation were raised to the utmost in the minds of all parties, to hear the argument of Otis, which he began in the following manner.*

"MAY IT PLEASE YOUR HONOURS,

"I was desired by one of the Court to look into the books, and consider the question now before them concerning the Writs of Assistance. I have accordingly considered it, and now appear not only in obedience to your order, but likewise in behalf of the inhabitants of this town, who have presented another petition, and out of regard to the liberties of the subject. And I take this opportunity to declare, that whether under a fee or not, (for in such a cause as this I despise a fee,) I will to my dying day oppose with all the powers and faculties God has given me, all such instruments of slavery

---

* The fragments of this speech are taken from Minot's *History*, Vol. 2. It seems from the letters of President Adams, that they were derived from some imperfect notes, taken by him at the time, which were afterwards carried off by some individual, who "interpolated them, with some bombastic expressions of his own," and printed them in a newspaper.

on the one hand, and villany on the other, as this writ of assistance is.

"It appears to me the worst instrument of arbitrary power, the most destructive of English liberty and the fundamental principles of law, that ever was found in an English law book. I must therefore beg your honours' patience and attention to the whole range of an argument, that may perhaps appear uncommon in many things, as well as to points of learning that are more remote and unusual: that the whole tendency of my design may the more easily be perceived, the conclusions better descend, and the force of them be better felt. I shall not think much of my pains in this cause, as I engaged in it from principle. I was solicited to argue this cause as Advocate General; and because I would not, I have been charged with desertion from my office. To this charge I can give a very sufficient answer. I renounced that office, and I argue this cause from the same principle; and I argue it with the greater pleasure, as it is in favour of British liberty, at a time when we hear the greatest monarch upon earth declaring from his throne, that he glories in the name of Briton, and that the privileges of his people are dearer to him than the most valuable prerogatives of his crown; and it is in opposition to a kind of power, the exercise of which in former periods of English history, cost one King of England his head, and another his throne. I have taken more pains in this cause, than I ever will take again, although my engaging in this and another popular cause has raised much resentment. But I think I can sincerely declare, that I cheerfully submit myself to every odious name for conscience sake: and from my soul I despise all those, whose guilt, malice, or folly has made them my foes. Let the consequences be what they will, I am determined to proceed. The only principles of public conduct, that are worthy of a gentleman or a man, are to sacrifice estate, ease, health, and applause, and even life, to the sacred calls of his country.

"These manly sentiments, in private life, make the good citizen; in public life, the patriot and the hero. I do not say, that when brought to the test, I shall be invincible. I pray God I may never be brought to the melancholy trial, but if ever I should, it will be then known how far I can reduce to practice, principles, which I know to be founded in truth. In the mean time I will proceed to the subject of this writ."

It appears that some of these writs had been issued, though by what authority is not stated; and the officers of the revenue were afraid to make use of them, unless they could obtain the sanction of the superior court, which had led to the application. It is impossible to devise a more outrageous and unlimited instrument of tyranny, than this proposed writ:[*] and it cannot be wondered at, that such an alarm should have been created, when it is considered to what enormous abuses such a process might have led. The following paragraph from the report of Otis' speech before quoted, will serve to shew what kind of instrument was here prayed for, and some results that might have been expected from it.

"Your Honours will find in the old books concerning the office of a Justice of the Peace, precedents of general warrants to search suspected houses. But in more modern books, you will find only special warrants to search such and such houses, specially named, in which the complainant has before sworn that he suspects his goods are concealed; and will find it adjudged, that special warrants only, are legal. In the same manner I rely on it, that the writ prayed for in this petition, being general, is illegal. It is a power, that places the liberty of every man in the hands of every petty officer. I say I admit that special writs of assistance, to search special places, may be granted to certain persons on oath; but I deny that the writ now prayed for can be granted, for I beg leave to make some observations on the writ itself, before I proceed to other acts of Parliament. In the first place, the writ is universal, being directed 'to all and singular Justices, Sheriffs, Constables, and all other officers and subjects;' so that, in short, it is directed to every subject in the King's dominions. Every one with this writ may be a tyrant in a legal manner, also may control, imprison, or murder any one within the realm. In the next place, it is perpetual, there is no return. A man is accountable to no person for his doings. Every man

---

[*] "The form of this writ, was no where to be found; in no statute, no law book, no volume of entries; neither in Rastall, Coke, or Fitzherbert, nor even in the Instructor Clericalis, or Burns Justice. Where then was it to be found? No where, but in the imagination or invention, of Boston Custom House Officers, Royal Governors, West India Planters, or Naval Commanders." — President Adams's Letters.

may reign secure in his petty tyranny, and spread terror and desolation around him, until the trump of the archangel shall excite different emotions in his soul. In the third place, a person with this writ, in the day time, may enter all houses, shops, &c. at will, and command all to assist him. Fourthly, by this writ, not only deputies, &c. but even their menial servants, are allowed to lord it over us. What is this but to have the curse of Canaan with a witness on us; to be the servant of servants, the most despicable of God's creation? Now one of the most essential branches of English liberty is the freedom of one's house. A man's house is his castle; and whilst he is quiet, he is as well guarded as a prince in his castle. This writ, if it should be declared legal, would totally annihilate this privilege. Custom-house officers may enter our houses when they please; we are commanded to permit their entry. Their menial servants may enter, may break locks, bars, and every thing in their way: and whether they break through malice or revenge, no man, no court, can inquire. Bare suspicion without oath is sufficient. This wanton exercise of this power is not a chimerical suggestion of a heated brain. I will mention some facts. Mr. Pew had one of these writs, and when Mr. Ware succeeded him, he endorsed this writ over to Mr. Ware: so that, these writs are negotiable from one officer to another; and so your Honours have no opportunity of judging the persons to whom this vast power is delegated. Another instance is this: Mr. Justice Walley had called this same Mr. Ware before him, by a constable, to answer for a breach of the sabbath-day acts, or that of profane swearing. As soon as he had finished, Mr. Ware asked him if he had done. He replied, Yes. Well then, said Mr. Ware, I will shew you a little of my power. I command you to permit me to search your house for uncustomed goods; and went on to search the house from the garret to the cellar; and then served the constable in the same manner! But to shew another absurdity in this writ, if it should be established, I insist upon it every person by the 14th Charles second, has this power as well as the Custom-House officers. The words are, "it shall be lawful for any person or persons authorized, &c." "What a scene does this open! Every man prompted by revenge, ill humour, or wantonness to inspect the inside of his neighbour's house, may get a writ of assistance. Others will ask it from self-defence; one arbitrary exertion will provoke another, until society be involved in tumult and in blood."

His argument in this cause lasted between four and five hours, and the summary of it can be best, and can now be only given, in the words of President Adams, who divides it into five parts as follows: 1. "He began with an exordium, containing an apology for his resignation of the office of advocate general in the court of admiralty; and for his appearance in that cause in opposition to the crown, and in favour of the town of Boston, and the merchants of Boston and Salem.

2. "A dissertation on the rights of man in a state of nature. He asserted, that every man, merely natural, was an independent sovereign, subject to no law, but the law written on his heart, and revealed to him by his Maker, in the constitution of his nature, and the inspiration of his understanding and his conscience. His right to his life, his liberty, no created being could rightfully contest. Nor was his right to his property less incontestible. The club that he had snapped from a tree, for a staff or for defence, was his own. His bow and arrow were his own; if by a pebble he had killed a partridge or a squirrel, it was his own. No creature, man or beast, had a right to take it from him. If he had taken an eel, or a smelt, or a sculpin, it was his property. In short, he sported upon this topic with as much wit and humour, and at the same time with so much indisputable truth and reason, that he was not less entertaining than instructive. He asserted, that these rights were inherent and inalienable. That they never could be surrendered or alienated, but by ideots or madmen, and all the acts of ideots [idiots] and lunatics were void, and not obligatory, by all the laws of God and man. Nor were the poor negroes forgotten. Not a Quaker in Philadelphia, or Mr. Jefferson of Virginia, ever asserted the rights of negroes in stronger terms. Young as I was, and ignorant as I was, I shuddered at the doctrine he taught; and I have all my life shuddered, and still shudder, at the consequences that may be drawn from such premises. Shall we say, that the rights of masters and servants clash, and can be decided only by force. I adore the ideal of gradual abolitions! but who shall decide how fast or how slowly these abolitions shall be made?

3. "From individual independence he proceeded to association. If it was inconsistent with the dignity of human nature to say, that men were gregarious animals, like wild geese, it surely could offend no delicacy to say, they were social animals by nature; that there were natural sympathies, and above all, the sweet attraction of the sexes, which must soon draw them together in little groups, and by degrees in larger congregations, for mutual assistance and defence. And this must have happened before any formal covenant, by express words or signs, was concluded. When general councils and deliberations commenced, the objects could be no other than the mutual defence and security of every individual for his life, his liberty, and his property. To suppose them to have surrendered these in any other way, than by equal rules and general consent, was to suppose them ideots [idiots] or madmen, whose acts were never binding. To suppose them surprised by fraud, or compelled by force into any other compact, such fraud and such force could confer no obligation. Every man had a right to trample it under foot whenever he pleased. In short, he asserted these rights to be derived only from nature, and the author of nature; that they were inherent, inalienable, and indefeasible by any laws, pacts, contracts, covenants, or stipulations, which man could devise.

4. "These principles and these rights were wrought into the English constitution, as fundamental laws. And under this head he went back to the old Saxon laws, and to Magna Charta, and the fifty confirmations of it in parliament, and the executions ordained against the violators of it, and the national vengeance which had been taken on them from time to time, down to the Jameses and Charleses; and to the petition of rights and the bill of rights, and the revolution. He asserted, that the security of these rights to life, liberty and property, had been the object of all those struggles against arbitrary power, temporal and spiritual, civil and political, military and ecclesiastical, in every age. He asserted, that our ancestors, as British subjects, and we, their descendants, as British subjects, were entitled to all those rights, by the British constitution, as well as by the law of nature, and our provincial charter, as much as any inhabitant of London or Bristol, or any part of England; and were not to be cheated out of them by any phantom of "virtual representation," or any

other fiction of law or politics, or any monkish trick of deceit and hypocrisy.

5. "He then examined the acts of trade, one by one, and demonstrated, that if they were considered as revenue laws, they destroyed all our security of property, liberty, and life, every right of nature, and the English constitution, and the charter of the province. Here he considered the distinction between "external and internal taxes," at that time a popular and common place distinction. But he asserted that there was no such distinction in theory, or upon any principle but "necessity." The necessity that the commerce of the empire should be under one direction, was obvious. The Americans had been so sensible of this necessity, that they had connived at the distinction between external and internal taxes, and had submitted to the acts of trade as regulations of commerce, but never as taxations, or revenue laws. Nor had the British government, till now, ever dared to attempt to enforce them as taxations or revenue laws. They had laid dormant in that character for a century almost. The navigation act he allowed to be binding upon us, because we had consented to it by our own legislature. Here he gave a history of the navigation act of the first of Charles II., a plagiarism from Oliver Cromwell. This act had lain dormant for fifteen years. In 1675, after repeated letters and orders from the King, governor Leverett very candidly informs his majesty, that the law had not been executed, because it was thought unconstitutional; parliament not having authority over us."

Taking a rapid survey of the terrors and vexations the colonists were exposed to under the reign of Charles I. and their tranquillity under the Commonwealth, he came to the first fruits which they tasted of the restoration, to the celebrated Navigation Act; and he dwelt upon this as the first in order, among those acts which were now to be enforced by the Writs of Assistance. The main provisions of this act may be comprised in a very few words; nothing should be imported into any of the English possessions in Asia, Africa or America, excepting in vessels belonging to the people of England, Ireland, Wales or the Town of Berwick upon Tweed, and besides being truly built and owned in said possessions, the master and three fourths of the sailors must be English; and no goods of foreign production should be brought even in English shipping, except from the countries that produced them.

He expatiated on the narrow exclusive spirit of this statute; but he would not deny either its policy or necessity, at the time of its enactment, because England was then surrounded by the power of France, Spain, and Holland; nor would he blame the conduct of Governor Leverett, and the Massachusetts legislature in adopting it in 1675, after it had laid dormant for fifteen years. It was a sacrifice they were obliged to make; but he contended, that the sacrifice was a very great one on the part of the colonies in general, and of New England in particular, and above all to the town of Boston. He thought this statute ought to have been sufficient to satisfy the ambition and cupidity of the mother country, who boasted so much of her indulgence and affection for her colonies.

The navigation act, however, was wholly prohibitory, it abounded with penalties and forfeitures, but it imposed no taxes. The distinction therefore was vastly great between this and the Acts of Trade. Though no revenue was to be derived from this act, still it was intended to be enforced by these Writs, and houses were to be broken open and ransacked under their authority to enforce it. The Writs of Assistance were thus extended in a manner, which had never been contemplated. He discussed most amply, all the effects, which the acts of navigation produced upon the colonies.

There are, it may be here observed, few statutes enacted by any nation, that have been more important, or excited more discussion, than the English navigation act. While the restrictive and monopolizing system was thought to be sound political wisdom, this act as forming an essential part of it, might be considered a masterpiece of policy; but in proportion, as wiser notions of national policy make their way into the councils of all civilized countries, and gradually eradicate the false and narrow principles of less enlightened periods, this act, which has been often relaxed in its operation, will probably so far as foreign trade is concerned, give way to the extension of liberal views in commerce; which all free and industrious nations find every day to be more and more productive of advantage to themselves, as well as to the world at large. Commerce is now gradually enlarging the prosperity and the rights of mankind; and wise statesmen begin to believe more fully, that the general prosperity increases individual advantage; and that nations gain not by depressing, but by a free intercourse with each other. This act did not meet with universal approbation at first, and in the language of Sir Josiah Child "some wise and honest gentlemen and merchants doubted, whether the inconveniences it has brought with it, be not greater than the conveniences." It is a curious circumstance, that this act which has been cherished with so much bigotry in England, and which inflicted so much injury and oppression on the Colonies, and especially on Massachusetts, should have originated from one of her own progeny, for such was its author, Sir George Downing, of whom President Adams speaks in the following manner.

"But it is high time for me to return from this ramble to Mr. Otis' quotations from Sir Josiah Child, whose chapter four, page 105, is 'concerning the act of navigation.' Probably this knight was one of the most active and able inflamers of the national pride in their navy and their commerce, and one of the principal promoters of that enthusiasm for the act of navigation, which has prevailed to this day. For this work was written about the year 1677, near the period, when the court of Charles II. began to urge and insist on the strict execution of the act of navigation. Such pride in that statute, did not become Charles, his court, or his nation of royalists and loyalists, at that time. For shall I blush, or shall I boast, when I remember, that this act was not the invention of a Briton, but of an American. George Downing, a native of New England, educated at Harvard College, whose name, office, and title appear in their catalogue, went to England in the time of lord Clarendon's civil wars, and became such a favourite of Cromwell and the ruling powers, that he was sent ambassador to Holland. He was not only not received, but ill treated, which he resented on his return to England, by proposing an act of navigation, which was adopted, and has ruined Holland, and would have ruined America, if she had not resisted.

"To borrow the language of the great Dr. Johnson, this 'Dog' Downing must have had a head and brains, or in other words, genius and address: but if we may believe history, he was a scoundrel. To ingratiate himself with Charles II. he probably not only pleaded his merit in inventing the navigation act, but he betrayed to the block some of his old republican and revolutionary friends.

"But where is Downing's statute? British policy has suppressed all the laws of England, from 1648 to 1660. The statute book contains not one line. Such are records and such is history."

From the navigation act the advocate passed to the Acts of Trade, and these, he contended, imposed taxes, enormous, burthensome, intolerable taxes; and on this topic he gave full scope to his talent for powerful declamation and invective, against *the tyranny of taxation without representation*. From the energy with which he urged this position, that taxation without representation is tyranny, it came to be a common maxim in the mouth of every one. And with him it formed the basis of all his speeches and political writings; he builds all his opposition to arbitrary measures from this foundation, and perpetually recurs to it through his whole career, as the great constitutional theme of liberty, and as the fundamental principle of all opposition to arbitrary power.

The first of these acts of trade on which he commented was the 15th of Charles II. ch. 7. in 1663, entitled "An act for the encouragement of trade" one short section from this act may be given as a type of them all, shewing in the most undisguised manner, the remorseless spirit of colonial monopoly. "Sec. 5. And in regard his majesty's plantations beyond the seas are inhabited and peopled by his subjects of this his kingdom of England, for the maintaining a greater correspondence and kindness between them, and keeping them yet more beneficial and advantageous unto it, in the further employment and increase of English shipping and seamen, vent of English woollen and other manufactures and commodities, rendering the navigation to and from the same, more cheap and safe, and making this kingdom a staple, not only of the commodities of these plantations, but also of the commodities of other countries and places, for the supplying of them; and it being the usage of other nations to keep their plantations' trade to themselves." — The statute then goes on to enact that nothing shall be imported or exported from the Colonies, except from or to "England, Wales, or the Town of Berwick upon Tweed." It may be imagined from the ardent character of the speaker, what must have been the tone of his observations on these ordinances. Mr. Adams says, that "some of them appeared to me at the time, young as I was, bitter."

The main question constantly recurred, where is the authority for the writs of assistance? After all the search that had been made by all the members of the bar who had been employed on either side, the only instance where the words could be found, was in a statute of the 13th and 14th of Charles the second, which was cited by Mr. Gridley, and which Otis denied to be either authority or precedent, or to have the least colour of either, in America. The statute was entitled, "An act to prevent frauds, and regulating abuses in his majesty's customs"; and in the fifth section, which had reference to prohibited or uncustomed goods being found on board of vessels after clearance, or in any place on shore, it is provided for the seizure of those goods, that, "it shall be lawful to or for, any person or persons, authorized by *writ of assistance under the seal of his majesty's Court of Exchequer*, to take a constable, headborough, or other public officer, inhabiting near unto the place, and in the day time to enter, and go into any house, shop, cellar, warehouse, or room, or other place; and in case of resistance, to break open doors, chests, trunks, and other package, there to seize and from thence bring, any kind of goods or merchandize whatsoever prohibited and uncustomed, and to put and secure the same, in his majesty's storehouse in the port next to the place where such seizure shall be made." Another act was cited in connection with this, that was passed in the seventh and eighth of William the third, chap. 23d. "to regulate the plantation trade." — This statute expressly recited the act before mentioned of Charles II. which it went to inforce, and that "like assistance" should be given to the officers as in the act of Charles — the word *assistance* here occurs for the second, and last time, in any statute.

But in the former of these acts, and in the latter, if the construction can be allowed to authorize a writ of assistance, these writs were to be issued under the seal of the Court of Exchequer, and were returnable to it. Otis, after alluding to both these acts, asked with triumphant confidence, "where is your seal of his majesty's Court of Exchequer, and, what has the Court of Exchequer to do here?" They had no warrant from the Exchequer in England, and could not assume to have any. It could not be pretended that the Superior Court of Judicature, court of assize and general goal [gaol] delivery in the Massachusetts Bay, had all the powers of the Court of Exchequer in England and could issue warrants like that Court. No custom house officer dared say it, or instruct his counsel to say it. This Court, it is true, was invested with all the power of the Court of King's bench, common pleas and exchequer in England; but this power was given by a law of the provincial legislature, by virtue of the powers vested in it by the charter. Yet neither Hutchinson nor the other judges, dared say that this Court was his majesty's court of exchequer, because the principle would have been fatal to parliamentary pretensions.

Otis went still further than to deny the jurisdiction of the court of exchequer; its warrants and writs were never seen here, or if they were, would be only waste paper. Such a "writ of assistance" he said, might become the reign of Charles the second of England, and he would not dispute the taste of the parliament of England in passing such an act, nor the people of England in submitting to it, but it was not calculated for the meridian of this country. He insisted further, that these warrants and writs were even in England inconsistent with the fundamental laws, the natural and constitutional rights of the subjects. If, however, it would please the people of England, he might admit that they were legal there, but not here.

The case of the petitioners was attempted to be made out, by a series of inferences and forced constructions of the most sophistical kind; whenever they could find the word "writ" or "continued" or "assistance" or the words "court of exchequer," they produced the statute, though it might be in express terms, "restricted to the realm." There were several acts of this kind passed under the Stuart kings, which were brought forward. Among these were, "an act for the regulation of the trade of Bay making, in the Dutch Hall in Colchester" — and an "act for the regulating the making of Kidderminster stuffs." There seems to have been no other reason for citing these statutes than their having contained permission "to enter, search, break open houses, shops, cellars, rooms, casks, boxes," &c. &c. and to seize and carry away "certain obnoxious articles." These odious and violent enactments, which have at all times perhaps, been too readily passed in England, were yet limited to some particular manufacture, which they were designed to encourage. Many of them were brought from different reigns, in which the rights of the subject were treated with little ceremony, in favour of establishing particular manufactures, and of destroying foreign rivalship, yet all these acts were confined to the realm, and their operation to very narrow limits within it. "The wit, the humour, the irony, the satire played off, by Mr. Otis, in his observations on these acts of navigation, Dutch Bays, and Kidderminster stuffs," "it would be madness in me," says Mr. Adams, "to pretend to remember with any accuracy. But I do say, that Horace's *Irritat, mulcet, veris terroribus implet*, was never exemplified in my hearing with so great effect." All the statutes were noticed from Charles II. to George III. inclusive, that the crown officers thought could be made to bear on the question. In the examination of these statutes, and especially of those called the acts of trade, he illustrated their spirit and tendency, by many references to Child, Gee, Ashley, and Davenant, whose works on Trade, and the Colonies, were a commentary on these acts. He shewed by many sound and striking observations, how unjust, oppressive, and impracticable they were; that they never had been and never could be executed; and asserted what must have then been considered rather extravagant, though it was doubtless true, "that if the King of Great Britain in person were encamped on Boston Common, at the head of twenty thousand men, with all his navy on our coast, he would not be able to execute these laws. They would be resisted or eluded." When he came to the consideration, of "an act for the better security and encouraging the trade of his Majesty's sugar Colonies in America," passed the 6th year of George II. which imposed a very heavy duty on foreign sugar and molasses, and which statute contains the following language; "we, your Majesty's most dutiful and loyal subjects, the Commons of Great Britain, assembled in parliament, have *given and granted* unto your Majesty, the several and respective duties hereinafter mentioned," he laid down maxims which thenceforward became current enough. He demonstrated the importance of these two articles of molasses and sugar, the former of which, especially, was connected inseparably with the fisheries, with almost all the commerce of the colony, as well as its manufactures and agriculture, and he observed by calculation the great amount of revenue that would be raised by it. He further advanced principles, that must have been heard by his audience with very strong, but very different emotions, when "he asserted this act to be a revenue law, a taxation law, made by a foreign legislature, without our consent, and by a legislature who had no feeling for us, and whose interest prompted them to tax us to the quick."

The last ground taken by him in commenting on these later acts of trade, was their incompatibility with the charter of the Colony. He went over the history of the charters. "Neither the first James nor Charles could be supposed to intend, that Parliament, which they both hated more than they did the Pope or the French king, should share with them in the government of colonies instituted by their royal prerogative." "Tom, Dick and Harry were not to censure them in their council." Pym, Hampden, Sir Harry Vane and Cromwell, did not surely wish to subject a country, which they sought as an asylum, to the arbitrary jurisdiction of a country, from which they wished to fly. Charles the second had learned by dismal, doleful experience, that parliaments were not to be wholly despised. He therefore endeavoured to associate parliament with himself, in his navigation act, and many others of his despotic projects, even in that of destroying by his unlimited licentiousness and debauchery, the moral character of the nation. In pointing out the violent infringement of the charters, from Dummer's defence of the New England charters, he bestowed many just praises on that excellent work.

In thus adverting to the history of the charters and the colony, he fell naturally on the merit of its founders, in undertaking so perilous, arduous, and almost desperate an enterprise; in "disforesting bare creation"; in conciliating and necessarily contending with Indian natives, in purchasing, rather than conquering, a quarter of the globle [globe] at their own expense, the sweat of their own brows, at the hazard and sacrifice of their own lives; without the smallest aid, assistance or comfort from the government of England, or from England itself as a nation. On the contrary, meeting with constant jealousy, envy, intrigue against their charter, their religion, and all their privileges. He reproached the nation, parliament, and king with injustice, illiberality, ingratitude, and oppression in their conduct towards this country, in a style of oratory that I never heard equalled in this or any other country.

After the close of his argument, the Court adjourned for consideration, and at the close of the term, Chief Justice Hutchinson pronounced the opinion: "The Court has considered the subject of writs of assistance, and can see no foundation for such a writ; but as the practise in England is not known, it has been thought best to continue the question to the next term, that in the mean time opportunity may be given to know the result."* No cause in the annals of colonial jurisprudence had hitherto excited more public interest; and none had given rise to such powerful arguments. When the profound learning of the advocate, the powers of wit, fancy and pathos, with which he could copiously illustrate and adorn that learning, and the ardent character of his eloquence, are considered; and that the disposition to serve his clients, whose cause he had undertaken to defend gratuitously, was not probably lessened by the instant conviction that his family had, with a view to this very cause, been injured by the appointment of the presiding judge, and that his belief in the importance of the subject must have been certainly enforced by all the personal sacrifices he had made on this occasion, together with the obloquy and ill will of the people in power which would follow his course; and, above all, a deep foresight of the meditated oppression and tyranny that would be gratified by the success of this hateful application — when all these circumstances are recalled, the power and magnificence of this oration may be imagined. With a knowledge of the topics that were involved, and the fearless energy with which they were developed and elucidated, the time when it occurred, and the accompanying circumstances; every person will join with President Adams when he says: "I do say in the most solemn manner, that Mr. Otis' oration against writs of assistance, breathed into this nation the breath of life."

---

* When the next term came, Mr. Adams says, "No judgment was pronounced, nothing was said about writs of assistance. But it was generally reported and understood that the Court clandestinely granted them, and the custom house officers had them in their pockets, though I never knew that they dared to produce and execute them in any one instance." Minot's history says, "The writ of assistance was granted," and refers to the court records for authority: yet this was probably a mere form to save the pride of the administration; and as nothing was afterwards heard of this odious instrument, President Adams's opinion is unquestionably correct, "that they never dared to execute them."

6. Tudor's concluding Remarks — Chapter VII.

In addition to the deep anxiety, which such a question as that of "Writs of Assistance," involving so extensively, not only pecuniary concerns, but political and civil rights, must inevitably have created; this trial was also accompanied with a peculiar interest, arising out of incidental circumstances of a personal nature, some of which have been already mentioned. There were others very striking. Otis was the pupil of Gridley, for whose character he felt a high respect, and for whose instruction he was sincerely grateful: and he never lost sight of these feelings in the course of the trial. "It was," says, the venerable witness so often quoted, "a moral spectacle more affecting to me than any I have ever since seen upon the stage, to observe a pupil treating his master with all the deference, respect, esteem and affection of a son to a father, and that without the least affectation; while he baffled and confounded all his authorities, confuted all his arguments, and reduced him to silence!" Nor was a suitable return wanting on the part of the master. The same observer in another place remarks; "The crown, by its agents, accumulated construction upon construction, and inference upon inference, as the giants heaped Pelion upon Ossa. I hope it is not impious or profane to compare Otis to Ovid's Jupiter; but, *misso fulmine fregit Olympum, et excussit subjecto Pelio Ossam.* He dashed this whole building to pieces, and scattered the pulverized atoms to the four winds; and no judge, lawyer, or crown officer dared to say, why do ye so?"

"In plain English, by cool, patient comparison of the phraseology of these statutes, their several provisions, the dates of their enactments, the privileges of our charters, the merits of the Colonists, &c. he shewed the pretensions to introduce the revenue acts, and these arbitrary and mechanical Writs of Assistance, as an instrument for the execution of them, to be so irrational; by his wit he represented the attempt as so ludicrous and ridiculous; and by his dignified reprobation of an impudent attempt to impose on the people of America, he raised such a storm of indignation, that even Hutchinson, who had been appointed on purpose to sanction this writ, dared not utter a word in its favour, and Mr. Gridley himself seemed to me to exult inwardly at the glory and triumph of his pupil."

An epoch in public affairs may be dated from this trial. Political parties became more distinctly formed, and their several adherents were more marked and decided. The nature of ultra-marine jurisdiction began to be closely examined; the question respecting raising a revenue fully discussed. The right of the British parliament to impose taxes was openly denied. "Taxation without representation is tyranny," was the maxim, that was the guide and watch word of all the friends of liberty. The crown officers and their followers adopted openly the pretensions of the British ministry and parliament, and considering their power to be irresistible, appealed to the selfishness of those who might be expectants of patronage, and to the fears of all quiet and timid minds, to adopt a blind submission, as the only safe or reasonable alternative. Otis took the side of his country, and as has been shewn, under circumstances that made his decision irrevocable. He was transferred at once from the ranks of private life, not merely to take the side, but to be the guide and leader of his country, in opposition to the designs of the British ministry. "Although" says President Adams, "Mr. Otis had never before interfered in public affairs, his exertions on this single occasion secured him a commanding popularity with the friends of their country, and the terror and vengeance of her enemies; neither of which ever deserted him." — Tudor's *Otis*, pp. 52-90.

PUNCTUATION
PRACTICALLY ILLUSTRATED.
A Manual for Students and Correspondents.
By KATE O'NEILL,
Of the Richmond, Virginia, High School.

16mo.   Cloth.   192 Pages.   Price, 50 Cents.

This manual on Punctuation contains all the rules and exceptions on this important but much neglected subject. The proper use of each point is practically illustrated by numerous examples in sentences so constructed as to show clearly the correct application of these rules.

Proper study of this book will do much to counteract the tendency to errors in the use of punctuation marks—errors that are so common, and that spoil so much that would otherwise be good.

The treatment of the subject is condensed and thoroughly covered. It will be found very helpful to all who write for the press, and especially to the large number of correspondents and stenographers whose letters should show a proper use of "points."

A FEW TESTIMONIALS.

"This is one of the best helps to punctuation that has been prepared for the class and the individual. It is clear, concise, well illustrated, and every way helpful."—*Journal of Education.*

"A useful little manual for all who write for the press, for correspondents, stenographers and typewriters. It is especially commendable for its clearness and simplicity of language and treatment. A little careful study of these few concise pages will do much to put the whole subject in a clear light, and will repay any writer who feels, as so many do, vague and uncertain as to what is really correct."—*The Christian Advocate.*

"A compact and useful little book which does not deal so much with the philosophy of punctuation as with its practical side."—*The Daily Times, Hartford.*

"We wish that every one of our correspondents possessed this book. There is more good sense in it on punctuation and the proper placing of signs to bring out the meaning than we have found in any other book, and they are so explained that the commonest persons can understand them."—*Observator, Huntington, Ind.*

An Academic and High School Arithmetic

FOR PREPARATORY SCHOOLS, HIGH SCHOOLS AND ACADEMIES.

By CHARLES A. HOBBS, A. M. (*Harvard*).

Master of Mathematics in the Volkmann School, Boston, Mass

12mo. Half Leather. 353 pp. Price, $1.00.

It is particularly well adapted for review and preparatory work, while the great abundance and variety of the problems are sufficient to give the pupil a thorough drill and render him master of the subject.

Special prominence is given to the Metric System, a thorough knowledge of which is required by all first-class universities and colleges, and its use is continued throughout the book side by side with the ordinary computations in compound numbers.

Careful attention has been paid to the selection of the problems, over a thousand of which have been taken from the entrance examination papers of various universities and colleges. A supplement contains 275 miscellaneous examples, all of which are taken from such sources, and from papers given at the United States Military and Naval Academies' examinations.

A FEW TESTIMONIALS.

"The book is admirable in that it is practical. More work and less theory for preparatory students is what I want. I like the variety and arrangement of the examples and problems. The collection of miscellaneous problems at the end of the book is unsurpassed in any work of my acquaintance."—*Prof. G. C. White, Southwestern University, Georgetown, Texas.*

"It is well arranged, with an unusually satisfactory number of good problems."—*G. M. Phillips, Principal of State Normal School, West Chester, Pa.*

"The author has made a book with which it is possible to give a review of arithmetic without requesting pupils to omit parts as being too simple or too technical, and without securing a dozen other books for suitable problems."—*E. D. Russell, Principal of High School, Lynn, Mass.*

"The book is giving great satisfaction."—*Washington Catlett, Cape Fear Academy, Wilmington, N. C.*

"The chapter on the Metric System seems to be unusually complete, and to be provided with a large number of exactly the sort of problems that are needed for college preparation."—*Edward H. Kidder, St. Mark's School, Southborough, Mass.*

Printed by Libri Plureos GmbH in Hamburg, Germany